Rugby Wit

summersdale

RUGBY WIT

Copyright © Summersdale Publishers Ltd, 2007
This selection was compiled by Summersdale Publishers
with thanks to Richard Benson.
Illustrations by Ian Baker
All rights reserved.

Summersdale Publishers Ltd
46 West Street
Chichester
West Sussex
PO19 1RP
UK

www.summersdale.com

Printed and bound in Great Britain

ISBN: 1-84024-608-1
ISBN 13: 978-1-84024-608-7

Disclaimer
Every effort has been made to attribute the quotations in
this collection to the correct source. Should there be any
omissions or errors in this respect we apologise and shall
be pleased to make the appropriate acknowledgements in
any future edition.

Rugby Wit

Quips and Quotes for
the Rugby-Obsessed

Richard Benson

Contents

Contents

Editor's note

History has been kind to William Webb Ellis but few can testify what his teammates thought of him when on a wet day in 1823, with complete disregard for the rules of football, he picked up the ball and proceeded to run with it. In the annals of time, however, on that memorable day, he will be forever blessed with inventing the honourable, brutal, but always beautiful game of rugby.

Amongst these pages you will find timeless quotes and quips by players of the game, lovers of the game and observers of the game. Be they profound, funny or just plain rude they all have rugby, with all its foibles and intricacies, at their heart. It's only fair that a game that has brought so much joy, so much passion and so much fuel for argument be given a platform whereby its players and fans alike can pass on their wisdom and their foolishness for all fans of the game to enjoy.

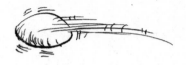

THE ALL BLACKS

New Zealand rugby
is a colourful game
since you get all
black... and blue.

Unknown

The whole of the world is tribal, but when it comes to rugby, New Zealand is much more tribal than most. The All Blacks are the national virility symbol. Their people support them come hail, rain or shine.

Mike Gibson, former Northern Irish rugby player

We are not calling them the All Blacks this week. They are New Zealand. New Zealand is a poxy little island in the South Pacific.

Scott Johnson, Australian assistant coach for the Wallabies

Of course it worries me if the All Blacks are invincible. I mean, it stands to reason, if we can't see them, how can we beat them?

Unknown English rugby player

❧

New Zealand are the best team in the world – the execution and accuracy of their skills were a lesson in modern rugby.

Josh Lewsey, English rugby player

You actually need
to see an All Blacks
jersey out on the
field, on the back
of the man who has
won the right to wear
it, to appreciate its
impact, its depth, its
sheer, unadulterated
blackness.

Unknown

I am shattered, our dreams were shattered and I feel sick about it all.

John Hart, former New Zealand rugby coach, after France defeated the All Blacks in the 1999 World Cup semi-final

You can go to the end of time, the last World Cup in the history of mankind, and the All Blacks will be favourites for it.

Phil Kearns, former Australian rugby player

Subdue and penetrate.

All Blacks club motto

—◆—

The suspicion is growing that the All Blacks will not have to be sublime in France. They will just have to be there.

Stephen Jones, rugby correspondent, sizing up the All Blacks' chances for the 2007 World Cup in France

Mud, rain, blood, haka. It sounds like rugby heaven to me.

Unknown

[It was] the first time I've ever felt like a boy in a man's body. I was absolutely shitting myself.

Zinzan Brooke, former New Zealand rugby player, recalling how he felt running out with the rest of the All Blacks for the first match of their 1992 South Africa tour at King's Park in Durban

Foul play and cheating are the two factors that can make the game unplayable... the All Blacks are guilty of both.

Clem Thomas, former Welsh rugby player

Five years ago, many of the England team were sick at half-time – such is the intensity of playing the All Blacks.

Lawrence Dallaglio, English rugby player

ALL BRAUN, NO BRAINS

That kick was
absolutely unique,
except for the one
before it which
was identical.

Tony Brown, New Zealand rugby player

It went well. There are no problems, and, as a bonus, it showed that I have a brain!

Corné Krige, South African rugby player,
after going for a brain scan

You guys line up alphabetically by height and you guys pair up in groups of three, then line up in a circle.

Colin Cooper, New Zealand head
coach of the Hurricanes

Nobody in Rugby should be called a genius. A genius is a guy like Norman Einstein.

Jono Gibbes, New Zealand rugby player

I told him, 'Son, what is it with you.
Is it ignorance or apathy?' He said,
'David, I don't know and I don't care.'

David Nucifora, Australian coach of the Blues, talking
about Troy Flavell, New Zealand rugby player

———◆———

I owe a lot to my parents,
especially my mother and father.

Tana Umaga, New Zealand rugby player

———◆———

It's definitely the hardest tackle
I've taken in my life but I'm still
breathing and that's a good sign.

Derick Hougaard, South African rugby player

He's a guy who gets up at
six o'clock in the morning
regardless of what time it is.

Colin Cooper, on Paul Tito, New Zealand rugby player

I want to reach for 150 or 200 points
this season, whichever comes first.

David Holwell, New Zealand rugby player

Colin has done a bit of mental
arithmetic with a calculator.

Ma'a Nonu, New Zealand rugby player

I've never had major knee surgery on any other part of my body.

Jerry Collins, New Zealand rugby player

It's not lost or anything,
we just don't exactly know
where it is at the moment.

**Derek Sampson, former New Zealand
manager of the Blues, on the whereabouts of
the NPC trophy after winning it in 2002**

Most Misleading Campaign of
1991: England's rugby World Cup
squad, who promoted a scheme
called 'Run with the Ball'. Not,
unfortunately, among themselves.

Time Out, 1991

BLAME THE REF:
EVERYONE ELSE DOES

Referees are only
human, I think.

Phil Kearns

Get off, you look ugly.

Peter Marshall, Australian referee to blood-spattered
Neil Back, English rugby player, after he complained
about being ordered to the blood bin in England's
2003 World Cup game against South Africa

I never comment on referees and I'm not going to break the habit of a lifetime for that prat.

Ewen McKenzie, Australian rugby coach

I think you enjoy the game more if you don't know the rules. Anyway, you're on the same wavelength as the referees.

Jonathan Davies, former Welsh rugby player

The first half is invariably much longer than the second. This is partly because of the late kick-off but is also caused by the unfitness of the referee.

Michael Green, author and British humorist, *The Art of Coarse Rugby*

Far be it for me to criticise the referee but I saw him after the match and he was heading straight for the opticians. Guess who he bumped into on the way? Everyone.

Ian 'Mighty Mouse' McLauchlan, Scottish rugby player

When a referee is in doubt, he is justified in deciding against the side which makes the most noise because they are probably wrong.

Unknown

A lot of abuse directed at the ref is self-explanatory – or kept simple enough so he'll at least understand it.

Justin Brown, New Zealand author, *Rugby Speak*

Referees aren't paranoid – everybody really does hate them.

Iain Spragg, British author

Grandmother or tails, sir?

Unknown rugby referee to Princess Anne's son
Peter Phillips, Gordonstoun School's rugby captain,
for his pre-match coin-toss preference in 1995

I never wore a mouth guard,
hated them... too uncomfortable,
and besides, you couldn't
abuse the referee.

Cliff Watson, former English rugby player

Often, when they're supposed
to be focusing on the offside
or forward pass, they're really
thinking about shoe sales and
chocolate brownie recipes.

Justin Brown, *Rugby Speak*

If you're a ref and you want
the big appointments, you've
got to lick the backsides of
some of the top nations.

Dave Waterston, New Zealand head coach
of Namibia's national rugby union team

I have been sent off that many times
that when I'm in the yard doing the
gardening and the postman goes
by and blows his whistle, I just
get up and go have a shower.

Noel Kelly, former Australian rugby player

Players and spectators at all levels
can enjoy sport better if they totally
accept two simple rules. Rule one:
the referee is always right. Rule two:
in the event of the referee being
obviously wrong, rule one applies.

Peter Corrigan, sports journalist

CELEBRITIES
ON RUGBY

My drinking team has
a rugby problem.

Oscar Wilde, Irish playwright, novelist
and poet (1854–1900)

Rugby is a game for big buggers;
if you're not a big bugger you get
hurt. I wasn't a big bugger but I
was a fast bugger and therefore
I avoided the big buggers.

Spike Milligan, Irish comedian (1918–2002)

Rugby – posh man's sport,
of course. Fifteen men on a
team because posh people can
afford to have more friends.

Al Murray, English comedian

I prefer rugby to
soccer. I enjoy the
violence in rugby,
except when they
start biting each
other's ears off.

Elizabeth Taylor, English-American actress

Rugby is a game for the mentally deficient, that is why it was invented by the British. Who else but an Englishman could invent an oval ball?

Peter Cook, English satirist, writer
and comedian (1937–1995)

[Rugby is] the most vicious sport on God's Earth.

Chris Eubank, English boxer

Rugby is a wonderful show.
Dance, opera and, suddenly,
the blood of a killing.

Richard Burton, Welsh actor (1925–1984)

Playing rugby at school I once
fell on a loose ball and, through
ignorance and fear, held on despite
a fierce pummelling. After that
it took me months to convince
my teammates I was a coward.

Peter Cook

Sweden and rugby aren't very good friends. I really don't understand it.

Sven-Goran Eriksson, Swedish former England national football team manager

———•———

Rugby is a good occasion for keeping 30 bullies far from the centre of the city.

Oscar Wilde

———•———

The women sit, getting colder and colder, on a seat getting harder and harder, watching oafs getting muddier and muddier.

Virginia Graham, American TV presenter, writer and commentator (1912–1998)

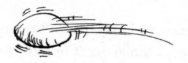

CLASSIC COMMENTARY

Strangely, in slow
motion replay, the ball
seemed to hang in the
air for even longer.

Murray Mexted, New Zealand TV commentator

Andy Ellis – the 21 year old, who turned 22 a few weeks ago...

Murray Mexted

Commentator: The Frenchman took a bit of a shoeing there, didn't he Brian?
Brian Moore: I don't care, he's a Frenchman.

An unknown commentator and Brian Moore, former English rugby player, during an RBS 6 Nations game between France and England

There's nothing that a tight
forward likes more than a
loosie right up his backside.

Murray Mexted

An easy kick for George
Fairburn now but, as everybody
knows, no kicks are easy.

David Doyle-Davidson, BBC radio commentator

Mate, that was bigger
than Hitler's gas bill.

**A replacement sideline radio commentator
after a state of origin match on how he had
found the experience. The station quickly
cut his microphone and apologised.**

What a great-sounding name. He
sounds like a drug dealer from Brazil.

**Murray Mexted, on Rico Gear,
New Zealand rugby player**

They trained like Tarzan all week
and then played like Jane.

Wayne Smith, New Zealand rugby coach

He's like a mad ferret.

Bill McLaren, Scottish rugby commentator

We want consistency, but we don't want a consistent referee to consistently blow the whistle.

Murray Mexted

You don't like to see
hookers going down
on players like that.

Murray Mexted

That guy is so quick; he can switch off the light and get into bed before the room is dark.

Jack Gibson, former Australian rugby coach

Well, either side could win it, or it could be a draw.

Murray Mexted

I look at Colin Meads and see
a great big sheep farmer who
carried the ball in his hands as
though it was an orange pip.

Bill McLaren

❦

The All Blacks second-rowers
are huge men. They're both
over one metre tall... hang on,
that would make them midgets.

Murray Mexted

If Walt Disney
had seen this little
man's antics, there'd
have been no
Mickey Mouse.

Ray French, English commentator, on Peter
Sterling, former Australian rugby player

Just watch the pace of the French defence. They are attacking the Irish defensively.

David Fordham, Australian commentator

Sky TV Producer: Murray can you hear me?... Murray can you hear me?
Murray Mexted: No.

A sound check before a Springbok test at Carisbrook

THE DRAGONS

Don't ask me about emotions in the Welsh dressing room. I'm someone who cries when he watches *Little House on the Prairie*.

Bob Norster, former Welsh rugby player

Welsh rugby may be about as healthy as a 40-a-day smoker with a gammy leg and a whisky habit, but Llanelli will be up for this.

Chris Hewett, rugby union correspondent, *The Independent*

Nobody ever beats Wales at rugby, they just score more points.

Graham Mourie, former New Zealand rugby player

Growing up in Wales meant two things to me: rugby on a Saturday and chapel on Sunday. The thought of doing anything else just never crossed our minds as youngsters.

Gareth Edwards, former Welsh rugby player

The job of Welsh coach is like a minor part in a Quentin Tarantino film: you stagger on, you hallucinate, nobody seems to understand a word you say, you throw up, you get shot. Poor old Kevin Bowring has come up through the coaching structure so he knows what it takes... 15 more players than Wales have at present.

Mark Reason, sports journalist, *Total Sport*

I knew he would never play for Wales... he's tone deaf.

Huw Davies' father, on his son's choice to play rugby for England

---

Wales have always had it in them to play this kind of no-fear, high velocity rugby, but it's not an easy trick to pull off if you haven't got the ball.

Martin Johnson, former English rugby player

I don't think they showed us respect as a team – but I think they will respect us now.

Graham Henry, New Zealand All Blacks coach and former Wales national rugby union team coach, after the Welsh defeat of England in the 1999 Five Nations

ENGLAND VS WALES

The relationship
between the Welsh
and the English
is based on trust
and understanding.
They don't trust
us and we don't
understand them.

Dudley Wood, former English
secretary of the English RFU

Look what these bastards have done to Wales. They've taken our coal, our water, our steel. They buy our houses and they only live in them for a fortnight every 12 months. What have they given us? Absolutely nothing. We've been exploited, raped, controlled and punished by the English – and that's who you are playing this afternoon.

Phil Bennett, former Welsh rugby player, giving a pre-game talk to the Welsh team before facing England

When it comes to the
One Great Scorer
To mark against
your name
He'll ask not how you
played the game
But whether you
beat England.

Welsh proverb

There is nothing quite like a
white shirt with a red rose on it to
motivate a Welsh rugby team, and
if the forwards indulged in the
time-honoured motivational practice
of butting the dressing-room wall
before taking the field, the ferocity
with which they began the match
(and indeed finished it) suggested
that the gate receipts would only
just cover the plastering bill.

Martin Johnson, the *Daily Telegraph*

THE ENGLISH

Turn them over.
Smash 'em. Simple
as that. Relish this
game. Relish it. Shut
their crowd up, shut
their players up.
Win the match.

Martin Johnson, before the Grand Slam
decider against Ireland in Dublin in 2002

I was going nuts. We kept putting ourselves in trouble, making error after error. But who cares what I thought? We have won the World Cup.

Sir Clive Woodward, former English rugby coach

They were outstanding. They are the best team in the world by one minute.

Eddie Jones, former Australian rugby coach, on the 2003 England rugby team.

Of all the teams in the world you don't want to lose to, England's top of the list. If you beat them, it's because you cheat. If they beat you, it's because they've overcome your cheating.

Grant Fox, former New Zealand rugby player

We're going to tear those boys apart.

Will Carling, former English rugby player, pinned this message up on the changing room wall before his team ran out to face the All Blacks in the 1995 World Cup semi-final in Cape Town. It only took 70 seconds for New Zealand to score their first try as they demolished England 45–29.

The only thing you're ever likely to catch on the end of an English back line is chilblains.

David Campese, former Australian rugby player

I will handle things the Brian Clough way. Whenever a player has a problem we will talk about it for 20 minutes and I will listen carefully to what he has to say. Then we'll agree that I was right.

Sir Clive Woodward

I could hardly kiss him, could I? We did realise we were hugging each other for a little bit too long, though – and moved on to find someone else to do it to!

Will Greenwood, former English rugby player, who was the first man into the arms of Jonny Wilkinson, English rugby player, at the final whistle of the 2003 Rugby World Cup final.

It was like the Falklands crisis. I was counting them in and counting them out.

Jack Rowell, English director of Bath Rugby and former England national rugby union team coach, on his multi-player injury substitutions against Western Samoa in 1995

Me? As England's answer to Jonah Lomu? Joanna Lumley, more likely.

Damian Hopley, former English rugby player

He was like Luke Skywalker in *Star Wars*, when he has his hand lopped off and keeps coming back again.

Jeremy Guscott, former English rugby player, on Jonny Wilkinson's return to the England side in the RBS 6 Nations

London salutes you.

**Ken Livingstone, English Mayor of London,
paid tribute to England's Rugby World Cup
winners by awarding them Freedom of
the City of Greater London in 2003**

The only hope for the England
rugby union team is to play it all
for laughs. It would pack them in
if the public address system at
Twickenham was turned up full blast
to record the laughs at every inept
bit of passing, kicking or tackling.
The nation would be in fits... and
on telly the BBC would not need
a commentator but just a tape of
that laughing policeman, turning
it loud at the most hilarious bits.

Jim Rivers, letter to *The Guardian*

The last thing we want
to do is to get too
close to one another.
We don't want to get
palsy-palsy. But if
we're going to have
a live session then
let's have England
against France
and let's go for it.

Sir Clive Woodward, on the prospect
of England training with France

They have this impression of English rugby that we all play in Wellington boots and we play in grass that is two foot long.

Sir Clive Woodward

You might see some pommies running around in sandshoes rather than studded boots.

John Muggleton, Australian rugby coach

FINAL WHISTLE

The time for
reminiscing is after
rugby. Then you can
sit down and get fat.

Josh Lewsy

I've always said I will play until
I am 30 and that is the target. I
would rather retire myself than
let someone else retire me.

Corné Krige

The only trouble is my legs
are not as strong as they
were. I can't run any more.

George Daneel, South African rugby player and
the longest living Springbok (1904–2004)

The heart is willing, the head is
willing but the body's had enough.

Keith Wood, former Irish rugby player,
on hanging up his boots

I simply adore rugby and still feel excited every time I pull on a jersey. That I will miss, and so much more, but I'm sure rugby has prepared me well for real life.

Thomas Castaignède, French rugby player, *The Guardian,* on his announcement to retire from the game after the 2007 World Cup

I was this guy who'd been racing around down there, on that field in 1999, running straight over people, scoring tries, winning games, having fun. And I ended up so sick I couldn't even run past a little baby.

Jonah Lomu, New Zealand rugby player

Being dropped
and Take That
splitting up on the
same day is enough
to finish anyone off.

Martin Bayfield, former English rugby player

My coaching reputation has probably gone up in smoke, but I really don't care. You want to cry for these guys. But at the end of the tournament I told them to go and get pissed and to be proud of themselves.

Dave Waterston, after Namibia were knocked out of the 2003 World Cup

Japan will give my body a chance to regenerate and hopefully by the time I'm 40 I'll still be able to run down the road.

Josh Blackie, New Zealand rugby player, on moving to Japan to play for the Kobelco Steelers

FOR THE LOVE
OF THE GAME

Rugby is just like love. You have to give before you can take. And when you give the ball it's like making love – you must think of the other's pleasure before your own.

Serge Blanco, former French rugby player

The women and men who play on that rugby field are more alive than too many of us will ever be. The foolish emptiness we think we perceive in their existence is only our own.

Victor Cahn, writer, *The Changing Room*

In this day and age of safety first, of seatbelts, and cycle helmets, low cholesterol butter, 'Warning: Smoking is a Health Hazard' – when so much is sanitised and safe – the opportunity to feel that sort of battle-knell thrill comes less and less often. But it is there in rugby, long may it remain.

Peter FitzSimons, Australian journalist and former Wallaby

Let me use an analogy. I have a Staffordshire bull-terrier. Every time I feed it osso buco, he eats it like it's his last meal, and I think I'm like, and the team's like, my Staffordshire bull-terrier. When it comes to meal times, that's how hungry, how passionate we are.

George Gregan, Australian rugby player

It matters not whether you play on some rain-soaked, mist-cloaked, winter field in front of 200 spectators, or 10, or even none, or if you play in front of 70,000 spectators at Twickenham. The sensation is the same – an exhilaration of the body and soul that will forever linger in the minds of all who have known rugby.

Fred Allen, former New Zealand rugby coach

Your throat is dry, your cheeks are burning, you feel breathless. All that stands between you and glory is an oval-shaped ball and a set of posts

Neil Jenkins, former Welsh rugby player,
Life at Number 10: An Autobiography

Tiredness and fatigue is a mental thing. The body is capable of much, much more than most people think. I love rugby. I can't wait to play. Stay fresh mentally, work hard at something else, and rugby is a pleasure.

Andre Venter, former South African rugby player

THE GOOD, THE BAD,
AND THE UGLY

The Good

American football
is rugby after a visit
from a health and
safety inspector.
Unknown

I love rugby because it's a socio-cultural experience; travelling the world and meeting people from different backgrounds... actually it's more for the frequent flyer points.

James Holbeck, Australian rugby coach and former player

Samoa really are an example to all of us. You had one team that had spent 350 million preparing to be here and the other nothing, yet Samoa showed what you can do with heart.

Rudolph Straeuli, former South African rugby player and Springboks coach

[Rugby] players can achieve greatness even in the absence of silky skills and talent because they are deeply courageous, indomitable of spirit, great leaders and can make up for technical shortages.

Stephen Jones, *The Sunday Times*

The Bad

Sure there have been injuries
and deaths in rugby – but
none of them serious.

John 'Doc' Mayhew, former doctor to the
New Zealand national rugby union team

Rugby may have many problems,
but the gravest is undoubtedly that
of the persistence of summer.

Chris Laidlaw, New Zealand writer, radio talk show
host and former rugby player, *Mud in Your Eye: a
Worm's Eye View of the Changing World of Rugby*

The only pain in
rugby is regret.

Unknown

I can't rest until I have tamed
the devil in my head.

Jonny Wilkinson, *The Guardian*

We're showing signs of getting
better. It's just a pity the
tournament is over now.

Kenny Logan, Scottish rugby player

People forget your good games,
but the minute you have a bad
game everyone remembers.

Faan Rautenbach, South African rugby player

Hell, it's been hard. I never thought
it would be this bad. You have
to be in it to experience it.

Harry Viljoen, former South African rugby coach

The Ugly

Rugby people. Can't live with them. Can't shoot them.

Tom Humphries, sports journalist, *The Times*

Two sausages at tonight's barbeque please.

Phil Kearns claimed he said this to New Zealand's Sean Fitzpatrick after barging past him to score a try and then making a two-fingered hand gesture

I may not have been very tall or very athletic, but the one thing I did have was the most effective backside in world rugby.

Jim Glennon, Irish politician and former rugby player

The winger resembles Mother Brown, running with a high knee-lift and sometimes not progressing far from the spot where he started.

Mark Reason, on Simon Geoghegan, former Irish rugby player, *Total Sport*

Rugby is like turkey. Without chestnuts it's crude.

Eric Poutal, artist

—◆—

Rugby people have always been college scarves and jutting jaws and silly songs I don't know the words of.

Tom Humphries

—◆—

If they're going to call you this superhuman player or whatever and you believe it, then you should also believe it when they call you a tosser.

Martin Johnson

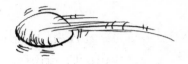

INTO POSITION

The backs preen
themselves and the
forwards drink.

Dean Richards, former English rugby player

Look, these *Phantom* comic swappers and Mintie eaters, these blond-headed flyweights are one thing, and we will need them after the hard work's done. But the real stuff's got to be done right here by you blokes.

Ross Turnbull, former Australian rugby player and Wallabies manager, talking to the Wallaby forwards before they played the All Blacks at Eden Park in 1978

I don't know why prop forwards play rugby.

Lionel Weston, former English rugby player

Prop forwards don't
get Valentine's cards
for religious reasons –
God made them ugly!

Unknown

Mothers keep
their photo on the
mantelpiece to stop
the kids going too
near the fire.

Jim Noilly, broadcaster, on the Munster pack

A good defender should be so mean that if he owned the Atlantic Ocean he still wouldn't give you a wave.

Morne du Plessis, former South African rugby player

The front row is an immensely technical place where brain and brawn collide; it is one which has fascinated me since I played a prop whose shorts caught fire during a game as a consequence of carrying a light for his half-time fag.

Bill Lothian, sports journalist,
Edinburgh Evening News

The touchline is the best defender.

Unknown

Playing in the second row doesn't
require a lot of intelligence really.

Bill Beaumont, former English rugby player

Props are as crafty as
a bag of weasels.

Bill McLaren

In 1823, William Webb Ellis first picked up the ball in his arms and ran with it. And for the next 156 years forwards have been trying to work out why.

Sir Tasker Watkins, former Welsh
president of the Welsh RFU

Forwards are the gnarled and scarred creatures who have a propensity for running into and bleeding all over each other.

Peter FitzSimons

***

If I had been a winger, I might have been daydreaming and thinking about how to keep my kit clean for next week.

Bill Beaumont

Rugby backs can be identified because they generally have clean jerseys and identifiable partings in their hair... Come the revolution the backs will be the first to be lined up against the wall and shot for living parasitically off the work of others.

Peter FitzSimons

You need a mental toughness and probably don't need to be too bright.

Mark Regan, former English rugby
player, on playing in the front row

THE IRISH

The Irish treat you like royalty before and after the game, and kick you to pieces during it.

Jeff Probyn, former English rugby player

It's a dismissive term to say the Irish team are plucky because it rings back to the old days when we went out and gave it a lash, set our hair on fire and ran after the opposition for 20 minutes and, if they survived that, they beat us by 50 points.

Eddie O'Sullivan, Irish rugby coach

Brian, what are you going to do for a face when Saddam wants his arse back?

Peter Clohessy, former Irish rugby player, to Brian Moore, during the first scrum of the England vs Ireland match in Twickenham in 1994

Tony Ward is the most important rugby player in Ireland. His legs are far more important to his country than even those of Marlene Dietrich were to the film industry. A little hairier, maybe, but a pair of absolute winners.

C. M. H. Gibson, former Irish rugby player, Wales vs Ireland 1979 match programme

Croke Park is more than a sporting citadel, however. It is a shrine, too, and represents the identity, culture and pulse of a nation.

Mark Souster, *The Times*, before the historic match between Ireland and France at Croke Park, Dublin in the 2007 RBS 6 Nations

They can talk the talk,
but they didn't walk
the walk, did they?

Richard Cockerill, former English rugby player, after
England's 1999 Five Nations victory over Ireland

Dublin and Lansdowne Road stood out for me – many a good win and many a good night was had.

Willie John McBride, former Northern Irish rugby player and coach, reflecting on his career

I didn't know what was going on at the start in the swirling wind. The flags were all pointing in different directions and I thought the Irish had starched them just to fool us.

Mike Watkins, former Welsh rugby player, on playing for Wales at Lansdowne Road, Dublin in 1984

LEGENDS OF THE GAME

Bloody typical, isn't it? The car's a write-off. The tanker's a write-off. But JPR comes out of it all in one piece.

Gareth Edwards, after teammate J. P. R. Williams was involved in a road traffic accident

I'm still an amateur, of course,
but I became rugby's first
millionaire five years ago.

David Campese

———◆———

The bone was out of place and
I could feel something wasn't
right. Fortunately, a few moments
later I went in to tackle Hull's
Steve Norton and my jaw caught
his knee. The impact caused
my jaw to click back into place
and I was able to carry on.

Roger Millward, former English rugby player

I love an inner calm, a coolness,
a detachment; a brilliance
and insouciance which is
devastating. Some sniff the
wind – they created it.

Carwyn James, Welsh rugby player and coach (1929–
1983), on Lions players Gerald Davies and Barry John

I'm going to leave it to the new
generation, to the crash-it-up
robots that dominate the game.

David Campese

His sidestep was marvellous
– like a shaft of lightning.

Bill Mclaren, on former Welsh
rugby player Gerald Davies

You know exactly what he's going to do. He's going to come off his right foot at great speed. You also know that there isn't a blind thing you can do about it.

David Duckham, former English rugby
player, on Gerald Davies

Youngsters need heroes. They need figures like Batman, Tarzan and Naas Botha.

Abe Malan, former South African rugby player

Gary should have his own comic strip in *The Victor* or *The Hotspur*. He's just an ordinary bloke, a lorry driver, and yet when he pulls on a rugby shirt, he becomes this sporting superhero. He's simply outstanding.

Jim Telfer, former Scottish rugby player and coach
on Gary Armstrong, former Scottish rugby player

A figure who inspires hero worship among even those who think a fly-half is a glass of beer consumed when 'er indoors is looking the other way.

Robert Philip, sports journalist, on
Jonah Lomu, the *Daily Telegraph*

LES BLEUS

The French are predictably unpredictable.

Andrew Mehrtens, New Zealand rugby player, after an All Blacks surprise loss to the French in the 1999 Rugby World Cup

Long after the match, when the stadium was dark, we all went out onto the pitch. We did a lap of honour, and we sang! We sang Basque songs for half an hour.

Serge Blanco, on the French team's celebration after defeating Australia in the semi finals of the 1987 World Cup

We will play well
today. Or maybe we'll
play well tomorrow,
we really don't know.

French Rugby Federation

They always lose when it matters.

Bernard Laporte, French rugby coach, getting it
wrong about England in the World Cup final 2003

If you can't take a punch, you
should play table tennis.

Pierre Berbizier, French rugby coach

The whole point of rugby is
that it is, first and foremost,
a state of mind, a spirit.

Jean-Pierre Rives, former French rugby player

As far as the English are concerned, I have decided to adopt the same attitude as them: I despise them as much as they despise everybody else. And as long as we beat England, I wouldn't mind if we lost every other game in the 6 Nations.

Imanol Harinordoquy, before France's match against England in the 2003 RBS 6 Nations

We French score tries because we cannot kick penalties.

Jean-Pierre Rives

We should have killed them off in the first half but didn't and paid for it.

Bernard Laporte, after France lost to Wales in the 2005 RBS 6 Nations

---

We didn't only lose the semi-final of the World Cup, we lost a complete generation of players. It was the end of that team. It felt like the sky had fallen in on our heads.

Philippe Saint-André, French director of Sale Sharks and former rugby player after France's 1995 World Cup loss to South Africa

I think the French always niggle, grabbing blokes around the balls and the eyes and that sort of thing.

Tim Lane, former Australian rugby coach

The only memories I have of England and the English are unpleasant ones. They are so chauvinistic and arrogant.

Imanol Harinordoquy, French rugby player

In the end at Twickenham, unlike at Waterloo, it was France who pounded longest – and hardest – as they lowered England's colours to bring the chariot to a shuddering halt.

The Sunday Times, on England's late breakdown against France in the 1997 Five Nations

LOOKING GOOD

It takes two hours
to get ready – hot
bath, shave my legs
and face, moisturise,
put fake tan on and
do my hair – which
takes a bit of time.

Gavin Henson, Welsh rugby player

Giant gargoyles, raw-boned, cauliflower-eared monoliths that intimidated and unsettled. When they ran onto the field it was like watching a tribe of white orcs on steroids. Forget their hardness, has their ever been an uglier forward pack?

Michael Laws, New Zealand politician, broadcaster and columnist, on the 2003 England pack that would later win the World Cup

He looks successful, regimented, invincible, and stuffed with certainties. It fulfils a stereotype of the classic English Man, the rugger bugger.

Simon Hattenstone, journalist, *The Guardian*, on Jonny Wilkinson

The rugger is an unlikely sex
symbol – a hybrid of jock, bear,
and the guy who might have
beaten you up in high school.

Christopher Stahl, journalist, *The Village Voice*

Rugby players are like lava lamps:
good to look at but not very bright.

Unknown

It's because of rugby I've
got dodgy ears.

Phil Greening, former English rugby player

As you run around Battersea
Park in them, looking like a cross
between a member of the SAS
and Blake's Seven, there is always
the lingering fear of arrest.

Brian Moore, on the England national rugby
union team's 1995 rubber training suit

LOSING

Rugby players may fall
in defeat but they will
never kneel for mercy.

Unknown

If at first you don't succeed, find
out if the loser gets anything.

Bill Lyon, American sports columnist

—◆—

We've lost seven of our last
eight matches. Only team that
we've beaten was Western
Samoa. Good job we didn't
play the whole of Samoa.

Gareth Davies, former Welsh rugby player

No leadership, no ideas. Not even enough imagination to thump someone in the line-up when the ref wasn't looking.

J. P. R. Williams, former Welsh rugby player, on Wales losing 28–9 against Australia in 1984

I feel like I am the captain of the Titanic.

Dave Waterston, after his Namibian team lost 142–0 to Australia in the 2003 World Cup

We actually got the winning try three minutes from the end but then they scored.

Phil Waugh, Australian rugby player

I don't know about us not having a Plan B when things went wrong, we looked like we didn't have a Plan A.

Geoff Cooke, former English rugby coach, after England had been humbled by New Zealand in the 1995 World Cup semi-final

Don't underestimate it, and don't assume it's a matter of simply going straight up. That would be naive and disrespectful to the opposition.

Stuart Lancaster, English director of Leeds Tykes, giving advice to teams relegated to National League One

It's bloody horrendous in League One, all graft and no fun.

Drew Hickey, Australian rugby player

—◆—

Ultimately you get what you deserve and we deserved what we got.

Paul Grayson, English Northampton Saints coach

—◆—

This hasn't been a very nice experience – I've got to slink home now in disguise because I still live in Bath. We got a stuffing.

Richard Hill, English head coach of Bristol Rugby

'If only' are the two most useless words ever uttered by sportsmen after a defeat but no matter how useless they are we still keep using them.

Rob Andrew, former English rugby player, after England was crushed by New Zealand 45–29 in the 1995 World Cup semi-finals

What hurts me most is some people will lose their jobs and that's hard to take. But the world keeps turning.

Paul Grayson, on relegation

OFF THE PITCH

It was not possible
for my players to
turn the other cheek,
as that was being
punched as well.

Eddie Jones, former Welsh manager of Pontypridd
RFC, on the 25-minute barroom brawl after their
1997 Heineken Cup game against Brive

I'm just off for a quiet pint;
followed by 15 noisy ones.

Gareth Chilcott, former English rugby
player, after his last game for Bath

We've been together three
and a half days and we haven't
been to the pub yet.

Donal Lenihan, former Irish rugby player and manager
of the British Lions, on the difference between the
professional 2001 Lions and his 1989 squad

I yell and scream like they do. I'm the worst of them. Totally. I'm a nightmare. Once they gave me the passport that was it – I started throwing my hands in the air, drinking red wine and flying off the handle.

John Kirwan, New Zealand rugby coach, on life in Italy

The use of video evidence is not always conclusive, but it sure beats the memory bank of most witnesses.

Jack Gibson

All three Tests will be televised and I've already re-arranged the lounge room so my armchair is at the front.

**Larry Devine, New Zealand father
of All Black Steve Devine**

———◆———

I've got a bottle of Johnnie Walker Blue. I'm going to consult it tonight and come up with a plan.

**Dave Waterston, following Namibia's loss
to Argentina in the 2003 World Cup and
preparing to face the Wallabies**

I'm pleased to say I don't
think about rugby all the time:
just most of the time.

Lawrence Dallaglio

———◆———

I think we would struggle to
get that one through.

Eddie Jones, on the news that South Africa
will subject their players to a 'no women, no
alcohol' policy during the World Cup

People think rugby players would make the worst dancers but you would be surprised. Some moves we use to warm up are similar to dancing.

Matt Dawson, former English rugby player, *The Sun*

The spirit was excellent. Yes, we were all naked together at times, but so what? The only chaps who were perhaps a bit shy initially were those with small willies. At times, we ourselves asked if we could strip off our clothes.

Unnamed South African rugby player after the media revelations about 2003 World Cup squad training camp, Kamp Staaldraad, South Africa's *The Star*

ON THE PITCH

The first half will be even. The second half will be even harder.

Terry Holmes, former Welsh rugby player

We can beat Ireland.

Pierre Berbizier, ahead of a crucial RBS 6 Nations
game with Ireland. Final score: Italy, 24; Ireland, 51

————◆————

It's like when two boxers come
together. Some boxers find it
difficult against opponents that
you would ordinarily expect them
to find it straightforward against.

Frank Hadden, Scottish rugby coach

————◆————

Get your retaliation in first.

Carwyn James

141

We must set our marker down early defensively, not sitting back waiting to see what they do. We need to knock people over and once we do that our game ticks over pretty well.

Eddie O'Sullivan

In one match last year eight water-bottle runners ran on the field and gave drinks to the players when someone was injured in the first 30 seconds of the game. 30 seconds – hell they must have been thirsty. When I played we got a piece of orange at halftime, and if you were quick you got two.

Colin Meads

I suppose you can say I am
a bit old school. I expect the
players to go onto the field
expecting to play a full game.

Kevin Putt, former South African rugby coach

Today we're going to do it simple:
forwards forward, fullbacks behind!

Unknown coach

I like to get in one
really good tackle
early in the game,
even if it is late.

Ray Gravell, former Welsh rugby player

The tactical difference between
association football and rugby
with its varieties seems to be that
in the former, the ball is the missile,
in the latter, men are the missiles.

Alfred E. Crawley, author (1869–
1924), *The Book of the Ball*

Ray Gravell Eats Soft Centres.

Banner at Cardiff Arms Park, 1970

146

We give up positions too easily in
the first 10–15 minutes and then
start the engines up. I'd rather we
started the engines up at kick-off.

Eddie O'Sullivan

❧

Throughout the week I have
one side of me that does all the
preparation and resting and eating
well and training, then it hands all
that over to the second individual,
and that other individual is a
hugely competitive, instinctive one
who is just desperate to win. He
is a bit of a monster, actually.

Jonny Wilkinson, English rugby player, *The Guardian*

If the team don't score a lot against us then we have a chance of winning.

Unknown

—◆—

Once you're on the pitch, it's chaos. I find it faintly amusing, this view that some people have of the captain, clicking his fingers and saying, 'Guys, let's try plan B' and everyone goes, 'Oh God, yes, plan B'. That's bollocks.

Will Carling, *The Independent*

PHILOSOPHICAL RUGBY

The whole point of rugby is that it is, first and foremost, a state of mind, a spirit.

Jean-Pierre Rives

Rugby is not like tea, which is good only in England, with English water and English milk. On the contrary, rugby would be better, frankly, if it were made in a Twickenham pot and warmed up in a Pyrenean cauldron.

Dennis LaLanne, French writer

Never a step backward.

Melbourne Rugby Club motto

Talent is secondary to whether players are confident.

Jack Gibson

Rugby football is a game for gentlemen in all classes, but for no bad sportsman in any class.

Barbarians Football Club motto

Life's a game, rugby is serious.

Unknown

All we're doing effectively is chasing a pig's bladder around a field, but we still have the ability to touch so many people.

Josh Lewsey

Rugby players are either piano shifters or piano movers. Fortunately, I am one of those who can play a tune.

Pierre Danos, French rugby player

I'd rather hit the ball than be the ball.

Hennie Le Roux, former South African rugby player,
on preferring golf to the prospect of coaching rugby

What makes rugby so special
is that there is always room
for the smaller man.

Conor O'Shea, Irish director of academies
of the English RFU, *The Guardian*

PLAYERS ON PLAYERS

[He's] the kind of player you expect to see emerging from a ruck with the remains of a jockstrap between his teeth.

Sir Anthony 'Tony' O'Reilly, former Irish rugby player and current chairman of the Independent News and Media Group, on Colin Meads

I think Brian Moore's gnashers are the kind you get from a DIY shop and hammer in yourself. He is the only player we have who looks like a French forward.

Paul Rendall, former English rugby player, on his teammate

———◆———

I've broken my nose this year and I put my teeth all the way through my lip. This is not good for my modelling career. I said to Nobby: How can I be a TV presenter when my face looks like yours?

Robbie Paul, New Zealand rugby player, on Brian Noble, former English rugby player and coach

Dean Richards is nicknamed
Warren, as in Warren ugly bastard.

**Jason Leonard, former English rugby
player, on his teammate**

———◆———

I've seen a lot people like him, but
they weren't playing on the wing.

**Colin Meads, former New Zealand
rugby player, on Jonah Lomu**

I'm sure the lads will be glad to see him gone. There'll be more food for everyone else now!

Austin Healey, former English rugby player, on Jason Leonard's retirement

It felt like I had run into a brick shithouse.

Thinus Delport, South African rugby player, on being tackled by All Black, Jerry Collins

Fijian full-back, Waisele Serevi,
thinks 'tackle' is something
you take fishing with you.

Jonathan Davies

I would have liked nothing
more than to knock him out

Corné Krige, on Matt Dawson

Will Carling epitomises England's
lack of skills. He has speed and
bulk but plays like a castrated bull.

David Campese

He moves with the
elegance of a cow
on a bicycle.

Frank Hyde, former Australian commentator
and rugby player, talking about Noel Kelly

It does add a bit of spice that it is Leeds and it's quite fitting that I'll be playing in my good friend Barrie McDermott's last game. I'd like to ruin it for him.

Adrian Morley, English rugby player

I've never seen thighs that big before.

Kenny Logan, on Fijian winger, Rupeni Caucaunibuca

One person has to slow him down, a second has to knock him over. He's young, naive, and we'll put pressure on him.

Will Carling about Jonah Lomu

There's no doubt about it, he's a big bastard.

Gavin Hastings on Jonah Lomu

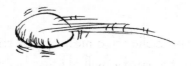

PLAYING WITH POLITICS

My favourite sport at
school was rugby. All
sports are teamwork,
but rugby particularly
is about teamwork
and I think teamwork
is the essence of this.

Gordon Brown, Labour MP

In the collective memory of this country rugby will always hold a place of pride for the role it played in nation building during those first years of our new democracy.

Nelson Mandela, former South African president

❦

World rugby has had a century of Lions tours, of invincible All Blacks and rampaging Springboks and where is the game of rugby in Honduras, Nepal and Egypt? Exactly where it was 100 years ago is probably pretty close to the answer.

Pio Bosco Tikoisuva, Fijian chief executive of the Fiji Rugby Union

Every moment paled into insignificance when Mandela came in wearing a Springbok jersey and with South Africa winning the final, it defined so much more of what the potential of sport can be; a healer.

John Eales, former Australian rugby player

It's like turkeys voting for Christmas.

Alan Solomons, South African rugby coach, on South African rugby administrators

I am prepared to back David depending on what his views are.

Glanmor Griffiths, former Welsh chairman of the Welsh RFU, on the appointment of David Moffett as chief executive

---

All I ask is that when people object to my ways is that they stab me in the front not the back.

David Moffett, former Welsh chief executive of the Welsh RFU, on his appointment

---

If the game is run properly as a professional game, you do not need 57 old farts running rugby.

Will Carling

A bomb under the West car park at Twickenham on an international day would end fascism in England for a generation.

Philip Toynbee, English writer and journalist (1916–1981)

Jeez, I've never met the president of a country before.

Malcolm O'Kelly, Irish rugby player, while naked in the dressing room after meeting Australian Prime Minister John Howard

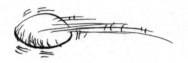

RUGBY WARFARE

I couldn't very well
hit him could I? I had
the ball in my hands.

Tommy Bishop, former English rugby player, when he
was questioned about his kicking of a fellow player

It will not be a Korean war, nor a Boer war, nor any other war. It will be 15 men against 15, it will be professionals against professionals.

Gideon Sam, former South African rugby manager

———•———

I mean we are lucky – people go to Iraq. He's not getting killed... well only for 80 minutes now and again.

Maile Falekakala, girlfriend of Moses Rauluni, Fijian rugby player, on the risks he takes

———•———

In rugby there are no winners, only survivors.

Unknown

South Africa were a disgrace.
Corné Krige as captain targeted
the entire England team. It
was all rather Jurassic.

**Stuart Barnes, English commentator
and former rugby player**

—◆—

The convicts will smash the toffs.

David Campese

—◆—

A player of ours has been
proven guilty of biting. That's
a scar that will never heal.

Andy Robinson, former English rugby coach

For an 18-month suspension, I feel I probably should have torn it off. Then at least I could say, 'Look, I've returned to South Africa with the guy's ear.'

Johan Le Roux, former South African rugby player, on taking a bite out of Sean Fitzpatrick, former New Zealand rugby player

If you're being poked in the eye or punched in the nose, you act accordingly. Some back off, some go for the blood.

Scott Gibbs, former Welsh rugby player

80 minutes, 15 positions, no
protection... wanna ruck?

Unknown

One of the first things to
understand about rugby is that it
is a violent game, sometimes it is
extremely violent. While violence isn't
the point (as it is in boxing or, say,
hurling) it is integral to the game.

**David Kirk, former New Zealand
rugby player, *Black and Blue***

You can't play well without suffering it, or being prepared to administer it. I'd go so far as to say that the team who can control their violence and apply it most effectively is the team that is likely to win.

David Kirk, *Black and Blue*

When he moved away and I saw the blood streaming from the eye, I thought, 'Oh God, I could be in trouble here.'

Martin Johnson

Thou shalt not hesitate at the breakdown, but be mighty to get your rightful ball; for though it is written that the meek shall inherit the earth, this truly was a poor translation. The meek shall be trampled into the dirt is more to the point.

Unknown

Rugby players have numbers on their jerseys because the coroner can't always identify the bodies by the dental records alone.

Unknown

It was blood-curdling stuff,
and English blood was
curdled to the point where it
all drained into their boots.

Martin Johnson, the *Daily Telegraph*

———◆———

At baseball games they play organs,
at rugby games they donate organs.

Unknown

———◆———

And there we see the sad
sight of Martin Offiah limping
off with a broken finger.

Ray French

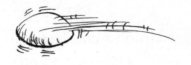

RULES ARE MADE
TO BE BROKEN

The advantage law
is the best law in
rugby, because it
lets you ignore all
the others for the
good of the game.

Derek Robinson, British author

There is far too much talk about good ball and bad ball. In my opinion, good ball is when you have possession and bad ball is when the opposition have it.

Dickie Jeeps, former English rugby player

Offside – a natural break in the play called by the referee every 35 seconds to let everyone get their breath back.

Unknown

You cheat and cheat until you get caught out and then you cheat some more, you've really got to play on that edge.

Brent Cockbain, Welsh rugby player

Half of the game of rugby is learning the rules, the other half is learning how to cheat.

Unknown

Thou should not kiss thy teammate on the mouth when he scores; for such is an abomination unto God, especially kisses in tongues, unless you play football with the round white ball and thus it is expected.

Unknown

Thou shalt not chip nor kick for touch if thou be a prop or wear any jersey number below that of 7; for this is an abomination unto the Coach, and surely you will be his at training, perhaps everlasting.

Unknown

THE SCOTS

Spy on Scotland? What for?

Djuro Sen, Australian spokesman for the
Wallabies, on allegations that they had
secretly filmed their opponents in training

Just like Scotland being gallant losers, we shouldn't apologise for winning, someone said we got out of jail, but who cares, we won.

Simon Taylor, Scottish rugby player,
on a narrow 22–20 win over Fiji

———◆———

I loved the Scots. Little Jimmy Renwick making a mockery of the centre stereotype... Deans throws, Tomes palms... John Rutherford and that sidestep. I always had a soft spot for Scotland.

Alex Goff, American rugby journalist

There is no man
more respected for
his abilities both
on and off the field
than this delightful
Scot, who is the
epitome of the rugby
man; brave, resolute,
adventurous and one
who loves a party.

Clem Thomas, on Gavin Hastings

The French pulled
up the Scots' kilts
and discovered
they had no balls.

Zinzan Brooke

Scotland is the Pacific
nation of Britain.

Va'aiga Tuigamala, Samoan rugby player

—◆—

Saturday March 17, 1990,
is one of those dates that's
engraved in my mind like it was
put there with a hammer and
chisel. Grand Slam Saturday
– the best day of my rugby life. It
was the day of the underdog...

**Gary Armstrong, former Scottish rugby player on
Scotland's historic defeat of hot favourites England
in the Grand Slam decider at Murrayfield**

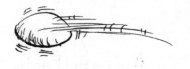

THERE'S NO 'I'
IN 'TEAM'

You have 15 players
in a team. Seven
hate your guts and
the other eight are
making their minds up.

Jack Rowell

189

I only get the points because I have
teammates who do the work and
put me in the position to get them.

Jonny Wilkinson

One thing that rugby is generally
is incredibly fair, and with it
being a team sport no individual
is bigger than the game itself.

Jeremy Guscott

Before the game friendship – during
the game is elegant violence – after
the game is rugby brotherhood.

Unknown

[Rugby is] a game played by fewer than 15 a side, at least half of whom should be totally unfit.

Michael Green, *The Art of Coarse Rugby*

Rugby is great. The players don't wear helmets or padding; they just beat the living daylights out of each other and then go for a beer. I love that.

Joe Theismann, former American footballer

Remember that rugby is a team game; all 14 of you make sure you pass the ball to Jonah.

Anonymous fax sent to the All Blacks before the 1995 World Cup semi-final against England

Isolate yourself if you want, but never alone.

Christophe Piazzoli, French rugby coach

UNION VS LEAGUE

Look, I'm going
to union and you
can't stop me.

Scott Quinnell, former Welsh rugby player

To play rugby league you need three things: a good pass, a good tackle and a good excuse.

Unknown

* * *

League is much, much more physical than union, and that's before anyone starts breaking the rules.

Adrian Hadley, former Welsh rugby player

* * *

Rugby league is war without the frills.

Unknown

It's the first time I've been cold
for seven years. I was never
cold playing rugby league.

Jonathan Davies, on *A Question of Sport*, talking
about returning to rugby union in 1995

❧

I'm 49, I've had a brain haemorrhage
and a triple bypass and I could still
go out and play a reasonable game
of rugby union. But I wouldn't
last 30 seconds in rugby league.

Graeme Lowe, former New Zealand rugby coach

If loving rugby league's wrong,
I don't want to be right.

John Sharp, member of the University of
Sheffield Old Boys Rugby League Club

~

Anyone who doesn't watch rugby
league is not a real person.

John Singleton, Australian entrepreneur

~

I like rugby league the most,
but I never played it.

Steve Waugh, former Australian cricketer

The main difference
between playing
league and union
is that now I get my
hangovers on Monday
instead of Sunday.

Tom David, former Welsh rugby player

The sooner that little
so-and-so goes to rugby league,
the better it will be for us.

Dickie Jeeps

In south-west Lancashire, babes
don't toddle, they side-step.
Queuing women talk of 'nipping
round the blindside'. Rugby league
provides our cultural adrenalin.
It's a physical manifestation of our
rules of life, comradeship, honest
endeavour, and a staunch, often
ponderous allegiance to fair play.

Colin Welland

Rugby league is a simple game played by simple people. Rugby union is a complex game played by wankers.

Laurie Daley, former Australian rugby player

Anyone who's seen the Wigan [league] players stripped has been faced with the raw truth of the matter... No time for male modelling, and even Princess Di would think twice about getting too close to that lot.

Colin Welland, English actor and screenwriter, *The Observer*

THE WALLABIES

What's with the Poms whingeing about the Wallabies whingeing? They do more whingeing about our whingeing than what we actually whinge.

Letter to the editor of *The Sydney Morning Herald*

Losing to New South Wales is like masturbating, or losing a golf ball. You feel really remorseful afterwards but you know it will happen again if you're not careful.

Chris 'Budda' Handy, former Australian rugby player

Good on you pasty-faced, transparent legged geriatric Poms. Your bunch of doddery old geezers showed us how test matches are won, and we showed you how test matches are lost.

Patrick Innes, Australian writer

Next weekend is
going to be a tough
one, whatever
happened against
New Zealand.
Australia are
a different bag
of hammers.

Eddie O'Sullivan

In every facet of the game, we're a bee's dick in front. Why have we Aussies won six of the last eight matches against the All Blacks? Because we're smarter.

Unnamed Wallaby in the *Sydney Star Times*

The impression I get from the guys is that they are happy to tour Europe, but certainly not Afghanistan or Pakistan.

Pat Howard, former Australian rugby player and coach

I once dated a famous
Aussie rugby player
who treated me just
like a football: made a
pass, played footsie,
then dropped me as
soon as he'd scored.

Kathy Lette, Australian author and
newspaper columnist

OLD GIT WIT

£8.99

Hardback

ISBN: 1 84024 542 5
ISBN13: 978 1 84024 542 4

You've made it. Old age. You want to make the most of your golden years and are finding yourself stereotyped and sidelined. But you're not the doddering geriatric people think you are.

Get inspired by this collection of senior sagacity and elderly erudition and show those young whippersnappers that old is the new young.